Cooking
with
Dogs

KAREN DOWELL

Two
Dog Press

Cooking
with
Dogs

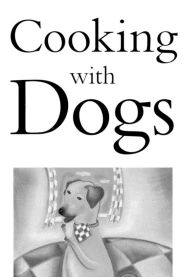

KAREN DOWELL

Two
Dog Press

First Edition
Designed by Lauren Smith

Publisher's Cataloging-in-Publication Data
(Provided by Quality Books, Inc.)

Dowell, Karen
    Cooking with dogs / Karen Dowell. —1st ed.
    p. cm.
    Preassigned LCCN: 97-91290
    ISBN: 1-891090-01-1

    1. Dogs—Anecdotes. 2. Dog owners—Anecdotes.
    3. Women dog owners—Anecdotes. I. Title.

SF426.2.D69 1998   818'.5402
                          QB197-41592

Two Dog Press
P.O. Box 307
Deer Isle, Maine 04627-0307
http://www.twodogpress.com

For Mike, MacPherson, Maynard, Scooter—
and Dave Duffield (who made it all possible).

Contents

If Dogs Could Fly...

If dogs could fly, would they lose their manners, hover over the stove sampling forbidden treats, ignoring the fruit bowl while nudging open the cookie jar, leaving telltale drizzles of drool?

If dogs could fly, would they soar through the woods, dodging branches, whirling around tree trunks, teasing red squirrels—or roll on their backs in mid-air and bark in pure joy?

If dogs could fly, would they pause before you, wagging as they stare into your eyes, kissing your face until your nose and cheeks are shiny with saliva, knowing you can't scold them for jumping up?

If dogs could fly, would they remember to come, sit, stay, heel, lie down—or just laugh because life is too cool to obey...

At least until supper time.

Cooking with Dogs

The kitchen is empty. You've gone for a walk, leaving me to cook alone.

No curious black noses glide along the counter's edge. No puddles of drool shine on the floor. No feet or tails to trip over. No nudges to remind me you like cheese.

I slice mushrooms in begging silence, set aside some chicken skin, and wish I were cooking with dogs.

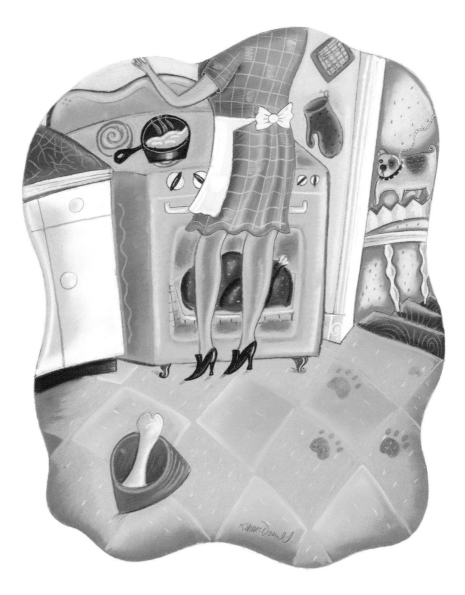

Animal Hospital

You wait at my feet, head resting on my knee, eyes filled with wet concern—anxious, pensive, contrite—as I stitch Betty back together. Borrow fur from retired tigers. Steal stuffing from extinct dinosaurs. Create a new breed of sheep to graze in your toy box.

You watch the needle fly in my hand as Betty's back is mended. Her left hind leg reattached. Her right ear amputated.

I inspect her sutures. Check her seams. Tug at her appendages— just to be sure. Then discharge Betty into your care.

You jump up, wagging happy. Take her gently in your mouth. Reverently carry her to your bed. Smother her with kisses.

And rip her to pieces again.

First a Dolphin

They come bearing gifts.

It doesn't matter how long I've been gone, where I've been,
they stage parades at the door. First a dolphin, then a frog, each
proudly held by a wagging dog. Their tap-dancing welcoming
committee promotes the wonders of home, so full of stuffed toys
that rattle and squeak.

And they beg: Why would you ever want to leave again?

Common Scents

(sniff)
 (sniff)
     ! ! r
       a   i i i i i i i i
         b b   t
                      t
                  t
             s
           q u   ?D O G! (p
             i   i   ?   e
            r   q u r e l !   e
          r e l s   r   ?   e)
                  ?
                t
              i
           b
         b
       e   r   a
     n
    n
   i
(eat) D

Dog on Drugs

It's snowing outside. He slinks, crouches on his bed. Petrified.
Waiting for the drugs to kick in. Those five generic Diazepam—
puppy Valium™ that will calm his nerves when snowflakes falling
trip synapses, translate into silent static in his brain. Who could
have known a January car accident would freeze frame, distort his
perception, so that winter scenes equate to quaking viewed from
inside out.

In fifteen minutes he'll be fine. A happy, well-adjusted dog. Playful
and mischievous. Eager to show off his stuffed frog. Until the
drugs wear off. The shakes return. And the phobias that haunt
him send him back to the counter where I keep his drugs.

It's going to be another long winter.

Dog Poets

They learn young to smell emotion—sniff around clichés to find
stories pungent with spirit. Yellow graffiti. Whiffs of e.e. in urine
scrawls. Territorial tales ripe with spontaneity.

Dog poets write, content with desire, to eat, sleep, procreate, play.
They breathe in their best work. And move on.

Sleeping Around

At midnight, you ask to come up by panting dog breath in my
face. You stare, insisting your bed is too hard, too cold, too lonely.

Loitering until I give in, you promise to curl up at my feet, then
forget—as you snore, grow larger than any dog in daylight. You
stretch countless legs. Jostle through canine dreams. Expand to fit
every inch of the bed. And force me to sleep around you.

Dogs in Kitchen

Food processor whirs—could be grating cheddar cheese. Poke nose up. Sniff. Ziploc® bags open—might contain sugar cookies. Act excited. Dance. Cutting board by sink—may mean raw meat and fat bits. Look intelligent. Frying pan on stove—chance of sautéed food falling. Sit. Stare. Drool. Plates out, table set. Good begging opportunity. Reposition. Wag. Storage containers. Eat scraps. Clean bowls. Check floors. Lick lips.

Nap.

English as a Second Language

We've been living together for almost eight years, yet he barely
knows the language. Content with his limited vocabulary, a
hundred or so nouns and verbs, he has no use for articles, adverbs,
or the nuances of tense.

He stares at me intently when I speak, waiting for the words
he comprehends, thrilled when he culls fragments of sense from
my exhausting sentences—even when the meaning isn't what
he hoped.

And if I don't understand his words, spoken with the intensity
of haiku, he, like a boorish American on vacation in Europe,
barks louder.

Shedding Season

Dog hair in my coffee. It's everywhere this time of year when my canine kids confuse outside cold and inside warmth. The dogs don't care. They casually discard strands of new winter coats into the air, around the house, faster than I can comb or clean.

Not that it matters. On this January morning, I'm more concerned about shedding extra pounds and old habits, resolving once again to be healthier, happier, and a better housekeeper in the coming year.

I'll vacuum later.

Seeing Smell

Fresh snow reveals smell. Transforms that invisible sense into tangible aromas encased in frozen plaster molds. Scents recognizable at last as dog noses poke braille trails of rabbit, deer, and red fox long gone.

Rawhide

You half-close your eyes, regarding me through slits of pleasure as you chew, massaging your gums, rendering your pressed, chicken-basted bone into a mass of sticky white goo that slides in and out of your mouth. Your jaws move—rhythmic, repetitious—your body frozen in a sphinx-like pose as you concentrate on canine oral sex.

The rawhide reaches the perfect texture—sinewy, slimy, slobbery—you swallow. Stand up. Shake. And beg for just one more.

Mud Season

The dogs have made their last snow angels. Winter's remnants
are scattered around lawns, like the dregs of a roadside yard sale.
Dripping, dirty white fabric frays in shade, surrounded by matted
carpet scraps of leaves tossed near the trunks of naked trees
sprouting prepubescent buds. The earth rots with thaw.

We're caught in that seasonal purgatory—on the cusp of spring,
riding the flicking tail of the dormant months across frost-heaved
roads that bump and thump eagerness into our eyes. Shaking off
the sleepy ennui of days too short to remember this magic vernal
ritual, the dogs waltz in mud, celebrating resurrection.

Philanderer

I can't see your face. Why do you run, disappear without looking back? Have I not loved you enough?

Who could possibly spoil you more? What could be more comfortable than sharing my bed? More pleasing than my companionship?

Your restless stare tells me nothing. Your brown eyes insist innocence, leaving me to imagine unsafe sex in shadows. Late-night snacks at Bett's Wire Trap. That crescent grin that signals when it's time to go home, and then...

How do you circle back, fall into my arms, delighted to be reunited, expecting unconditional forgiveness? And win it!

With a hot, panting kiss that reminds me you're just a dog.

Separation Anxiety

I find myself measuring gaits, sizing up smiles, angling for eye contact when we're apart. Sometimes, I confess, I've taken walks with strangers—just to hold a leash, feel that familiar tug against my authority, against my heart.

But it's never the same. They don't look at me the way you do. Other dogs only make me miss you more.

Tall Tales

Who was more surprised, you or that red squirrel, when you squeezed it out of its leaf-pile hiding place? What were you thinking as you held it in paws suspended above awe-struck jaws: Pet? Servant? Supper? A brush-tailed trophy to tack above your bed, to boast about to all your pals?

And why did you decide to set it free? Because the joy was in the chase and you wanted to play the game over and over and over?

If only you'd known that damn squirrel, forever criticizing your moves from the safety of trees, would never let you win again.

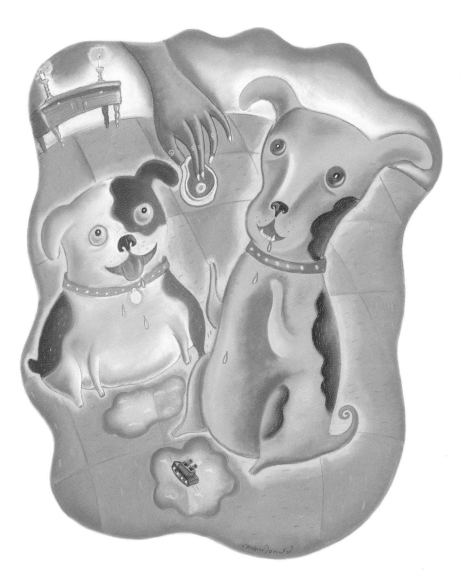

Food

One should eat to live, not live to eat, or so said Molière...
not that my puppies care. The musings of dead French play-
wrights don't move them as much as a well-deserved treat.

My four-legged gourmands eat to live and live to eat. Their
food obsession obviates presentation, focuses on ingestion,
ends in defecation with the simple, direct elegance of dog
digestive systems.

They never diet, except against their will. But they drool.
Standing in saliva pools, they wait for the next morsel to drop,
tasting it over and over in anticipation, almost disappointed
when their patience pays off...

And it's always over too soon.

Dog Phone

Last night before I went to work, I gave you a cell phone to wear around your neck like a high-tech St. Bernard. You were so proud—parading, poking, practicing, showing off your new toy. I taught you how to speed-dial 911, the fire department, my office, then explained about emergencies. You nodded and wagged.

But after I left, you forgot it all...called Domino's and UPCO, ordered pizzas, chew toys, and a jumbo box of rawhide. I returned to find your cell phone beeping and forgotten, discarded in shredded cardboard, and you, lying among pizza boxes, too full to feel guilty.

As I retrieved the phone, shaking my finger at you, lecturing about phone charges and irresponsibility, you kissed me awake.

Motherhood

All my friends have children now. Their biological clocks ticked them into a foreign world filled with bassinets and learning toys.

A few feel sorry for me, the last remaining nullipara. But those who know me best, and know my boys, know we share similar motherhood joys. Regardless of our breed of babe, we're both obsessed with the quality and quantity of our tyke's bodily wastes. And we delight in little miracles, innocent presents retrieved from beach and woods, random kisses, implicit trust, unquestioning adoration.

We teach, we spoil, we chide, we coax, we praise, we love our babies.

How can you feel sorry for a mom whose kids will never fall in with the wrong crowd, do drugs, or drop out of school? Dog moms are doubly blessed. Our boys and girls grow old, but never grow up.

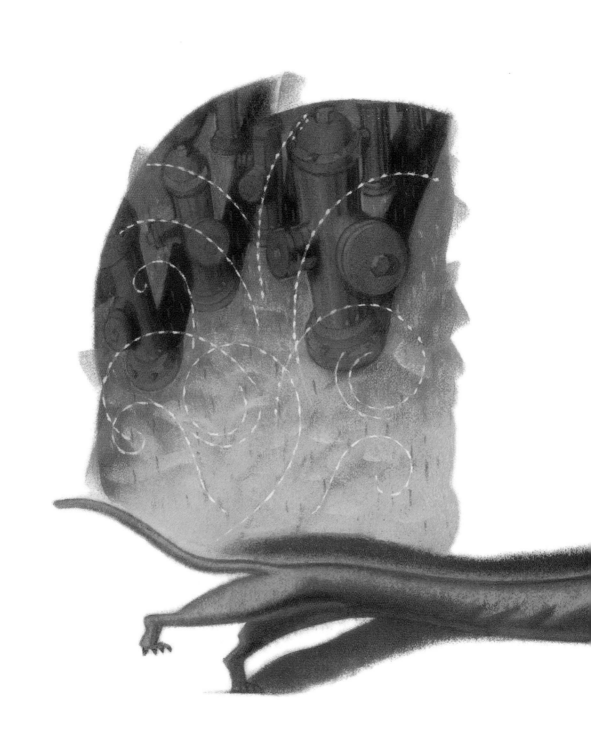

Last Walk

I turn off the TV, shut down my laptop, and you jump up,
skidding halfway to the door before you realize you're awake.
You stretch and bow, impatient, eager for your last walk.

But when we get outside, you forget how badly you wanted
to pee, suddenly obsessed with grass and tree trunk smells—
that woody bouquet of bark mingling with chipmunk, squirrel,
and fox scents.

I try to look uninterested, act unpressed for time as you nose
around, searching for the perfect spot to write good night.

And when you finish, you rush to the front door
and wait, wondering what's taking me so long.

Ghosts

Grumbling at moonlight. Your ears are tense with noise, triangles of attention cocked to catch sounds of leaves brushing eaves, acorns tap-tap-clacking the Morse code of ghosts. As spirit dogs stalk the house, your hackles rise with the moon, which traces shadows of creatures I can't see or hear.

I never understand what you're barking at when nothing's there.

Pedigrees

Buddhist monks once aspired to be reincarnated as Shih Tzus,
pampered emperors' dogs that serve as tiny watchers trained to
listen and wake big dog guards, then return to their soft,
shiny silk pillows.

My big labs would like a Shih Tzu or two to tell them it's OK
to bark, skillfully knead their broad backs and bellies with petite
paws, performing Shih Tzu shiatsu. Then, on command,
return to being soft, furry, puppy pillows.

Chasing Rabbits

A rabbit dons its white winter coat, unaware the world has thawed. Visible when it should be invisible. And it's driving you *insane*.

You want that rabbit. Those two ears hopping just beyond reach. That teasing tail tempting you into unexplored corners of the woods. Disappearing. Reappearing. Vanished.

You streak across the path, furiously wagging your tail, retracing your trail, a blur of frustration. Then slowly come panting back.

If you could talk, I know you'd say, "Tomorrow, Mom. Just watch."

Love Story

Mac met Disney when he was just a pup, barely out of obedience school. He'd never seen a spaniel before, a girl with spots and long hair, who'd let him chase her through blueberry barrens and spruce forests.

For six months, they courted, sneaking away for walks in the woods, skinny dips in the salt pond, romps in the meadow. Mac, with his bronzed big-boy looks, Disney, shining and sweet, they were a handsome couple, who loved to spend hours playing—nibbling each other's necks in a quiet corner far from owner eyes.

When Disney moved away, she never said goodbye. She didn't know she was being shipped four thousand miles to wait out quarantine in a British kennel.

Mac moped for months. His first love was gone. Her house empty. Her smell fading.

Seven years later, he still cries when he hears her name.

On Hold

No one wants to play with you. Toss your ball. Tug your rope.
Rub your belly. Stroke your back. Whisper love and praise into
your ear.

You've tried to win attention by butting against legs, sighing,
whining, barking—short, loud, authoritative woofs. But nothing
works. You're rewarded only with a sharp list of commands:
Quiet! Go to your bed! Lie down!

So you retire to your favorite corner, where you can see all
through anxious, alert eyes. Sink your head onto your paws.
Deflate to wait until you're wanted...or running away in
your dreams.

Going to Town

You take driving seriously. As though you know the facts and
stats about accidents and airbags—or bear some royal burden,
representing the best of your breed as you survey subjects from
the passenger seat.

There on your mobile throne, you assume an attentive stance,
an intelligent air of curious benevolence, charmed and gracious
when bank tellers and postal workers offer you biscuits.

But regardless of the pomp and circumstance you ascribe to
the journey—your dignity dissolves into spittle-spraying barking
fits at the sight of another dog.

Sensory Perception

Dogs see colors with their nose, sniffing out the reds and greens that brighten their monochrome days, searching for the perfect shade of smell to roll in and wear home.

Dog's Night Out

I can never tell when the urge will strike you, when
the siren song of the wild will drown the allure of
sleeping on the big bed with me. You disappear
into the woods under the pretense of peeing.
And don't come back. Even when I call your
name and rattle the bone bucket, your
rustling becomes faint, fading into a forest
of spruce and white birch.

You never say goodbye. You never tell me
where you're going. You never call.

Out cattin' around until dawn, you drag
home long after the dog bars close, bark
twice at the door, low and apologetic,
embarrassed when I glare. Too tired to
climb stairs, you collapse in the corner,
exhausted, like a college kid sleeping
off his first drunk.

Thinking of You

Lounging in the sitting room of an old Scottish croft house,
I'm reminded of you. This mildew-scented, spider-webbed space,
heated by the fake flames of an electric fireplace, could use a dog
to warm it up.

It's raining again. I see you in the faces of sheep and lambs
huddled together as they stare at stark Hebridean landscapes,
surf-licked sand skirts of misted hills and black mountains.

I snap my book shut, let my hand drift down to where you'd
be lying had I chosen a destination closer to home. And wonder
if you're pining in your kennel cell, longing for my return, as
I long for you now.

But I know you. You don't have time for homesickness. You're
too busy barking or strutting your male-dog charm as you vie for
the attention of some young *chienne fatale*.

You never remember how much you miss me until I pick you up.

Doghenge

It must be tough to be a working dog, trotting through life
without a job. Son of beribboned parents, hunting and field-trial
champions. Snatched from a glamorous world, condemned to a
life of leisure.

Perhaps that's why you're so intent on building these chaotic stone
fences of rocks retrieved from the shallows of Southeast Harbor.
You attack your calling with the passion of an artistic entrepre-
neur, selecting stones for shape, size, texture. Lugging them up
granite cliffs into blueberry barrens, where you seek the perfect
spot to deposit each one before going back for more.

You are possessed, as if you want your legacy to last long after
your teeth are gone.

Dog Days

Hot boys lie in bed panting. Personal air conditioners curled
on high. Bowl of cubes untouched. Too tired to chew ice. Too
breathless to bark at boats or UPS.

Hot boys basking in cool, dripping, summer dreams of swimming
with Gypsy Rose, the malamute stripper next door. Summer heat.
Summer love.

Puppy Nachos

I don't know if it was the margarita or your clamant stance
that made me shove aside chips to arrange dog biscuits on the
baking sheet. Slice thin strips of Monterey Jack to place on each
bone-shaped bit. Garnish each pet-mex morsel with chopped,
unspiced meat. Broil. Then toss them in your mouth in between
bites of my own Mexican appetizers.

You demand them now. At the sight of salsa jars, you want
puppy nachos.

Norwegian Shepherd

On a quiet lane along Sogn og fjordane, in the shadows of the
Jostedalsbreen, a Norwegian farm clings red against a hillside
plunging up from mirrored fjords.

In the fields behind an aging barn, a spotted border collie worries
his woolen-clothed charges as he races and paces to coax them
uphill toward greener pastures. He herds efficiently, nudging ewes
and lambs, barking commands with the calm self-assurance of a
professional shepherd. Until a Volvo buzzes by in a cloud of dust
and diesel fumes.

And he forgets his day job, jumps the fence, and disappears
in pursuit.

For the Dogs

They say that dogs have the same acute perceptiveness as small children. Subtle shifts in relationships make them as nervous as seeing a suitcase on a bed. They get edgy. Desperate for attention and the sanctity of their complete pack.

So I've been watching the boys. Even though Roger and I are tiptoeing emotionally around them, saving our more spectacular arguments for the commute to San Francisco, Toby and Gregor still know. And no amount of rubbing behind the ears or verbal reassurance seems to help. They feel the distance between us. Smell the stale passion.

Toby has begun chewing on baseboards and doormats. Something he hasn't done since he was a puppy. And Gregor. He perches at the top of the stairs, watching us like a predator. Peering down at our microcosm of a world centered around the kitchen and TV, awaiting death. Or maybe chicken skin.

Occasionally, the two of them gang up. Smother me with loyalty. Poke me with cool black noses. One on either side, each resting a chin on a corner of my keyboard, nudging my hands as I try to type, whining softly if I don't respond.

And they stare at Roger, lecturing him with solemn eyes. The eyes of priests that ask: "Why aren't you trying harder? You shouldn't run away. You should be faithful. Loving. Unselfish." That's what Roger says anyway.

Funny. The only thing we agree on these days is the dogs. And neither of us knows what to do about them. It may sound kinda crazy, but I'm more worried about them than I think I would be if we had children. You can reason with kids—lie to them more easily.

But the dogs? I've had these long conversations with them, to explain to them—maybe even to myself—what's going on. When I finish, Toby kisses me the way he does when I take his picture and the flash goes off. Trusting, but a little offended. Greg just shakes and walks off.

So...we're giving it one more shot. We've started taking evening strolls down by the reservoir again—me and Roger, Greg and Toby—together, as a family. It's been nice, actually. We haven't really done that since, gosh, four, five years ago. Yesterday, we even had a picnic. Fed the boys cheese sticks. Watched the sun set into the Orinda hills. Drank the last bottle of that Bordeaux my mom gave us for our anniversary. And Gregor, who's usually reserved and somewhat stingy with his kisses, gave both me and Roger a light lick on the hand, as if to say: "See, isn't this much better?"

It's a pity the dogs can't be with us all the time.

The Cooks

Karen Dowell lives in Maine with her husband and their labrador retriever sons. Dogs often wander into her short stories and prose poetry, without warning, and demand attention. Usually, they get it.

Lauren Smith is a graphic designer based in Palo Alto, California. His miniature dachshunds seldom participate in design meetings, but have been known to voice opinions during conference calls.

Illustrator **Marty Braun** lives in Maine. His dog Maggie is old and wise and, with two large black spots, graphic in her own way. Marty's work appears on pages 24, 30, 37, 53.

Illustrator **Greg Dearth** notes that people have always been a big disappointment for him, whereas dogs are in it for the long haul. So to Henry and Petunia, he says, "Thanks. Here's a biscuit!" Greg's work appears on pages 14, 39, 48.

Illustrator **Robert Forsbach** lives in Mesquite, Texas, with his wife and two kids. A few years ago, they coaxed a homeless terrier to move in. Buster now shares the Forsbach family with black lab Shadow and cocker spaniel mix Taffy. Robert's work appears on pages 8, 17, 54.

Dan May, who designed the dog and bone pattern we used on the cover and fly sheets, lives in Oakland, California.

Illustrator **Mercedes McDonald** of Toluca Lake, California, is actually a cat person, but a curious black and white terrier often appears in her work. She recently remembered that the dog is her childhood buddy, Zozo. Mercedes' illustrations appear on the cover and pages 11, 20, 23, 34, 57.

Mary Ross is a San Francisco-based illustrator. Her ex-dog Pepper (also known as Bad Bad Wuffle Brown) actually taught himself to open the refrigerator. He was not known to smoke cigars. Mary's dog "icons" appear throughout the book.

San Francisco-based illustrator **Ward Schumaker** likes to draw dogs because he has a cat. Ward's work appears on pages 29, 45.

Illustrator **Sally Wern-Comport** really enjoys drawing people. After all, she says, dogs are people too. Sally's illustrations appear on pages 41, 47, 61.